Cybersecurity Jobs & Career Paths

Book 2

Find Cybersecurity Jobs

By

Bruce Brown, CISSP, ISC2 CAP

Download free ATS resume templates at:

convocourses.com/courses/resume[1]

Check us out on:

youtube.com/convocourses[2]

Contact us:

contact@convocourses.com

---

1. https://securitycompliance.thinkific.com/courses/resume

2. *https://www.youtube.com/convocourses*

Hacking = Cybersecurity?

There is a lot of interest in cybersecurity, but people think that it's all about hacking. In this book I want to show you that there are many categories of this career path that have nothing to do with hacking or coding.

TV and movies glamorize this one aspect of cybersecurity and it's so ingrained in people's minds that they think that hacking is cybersecurity.

I have been doing cybersecurity and IT since the year 2000 and I want to inform you that there is a lot more to cybersecurity than cracking passwords, infiltrating a school's system to change the grades or breaking into the databases of banks and police departments.

Cybersecurity includes creating encryption modules, meeting laws and regulations of countries, and industries. It also involves intelligence and analysis of network traffic, analysis of software code and securing digital evidence for a criminal case. Because computers have to be in an environment that is controlled, cybersecurity also includes some physical and personnel security. You have to control who has physical security to the systems.

Cybersecurity is important for every aspect of information technology from the initial design of a computer system to a system's end of life. Computer hacking is a small percentage of what cybersecurity is. In fact, what is hacking? The Oxford dictionary defines it as the act of "gaining unauthorized access to data in a system or computer." This is a very limited definition of the term. What cybersecurity professionals consider "hacking" is a pretty broad field that includes, penetration testing, red teams, black hats, gray hats, white hats, phreakers, social engineering and others.

Cybersecurity is a huge field that requires more than just clever hackers who can crack a database. We need skilled communicators, leaders, managers, and analysts from all walks of life. Not all cybersecurity professionals are even technical.

With this book, my hope is for you to understand the breadth of opportunities available in the cybersecurity field by broadening your understanding of the term.

If you want to know more about cybersecurity as a whole join us on:

- convocourses.com[1]
- youtube.com/convocourses[2]
- convocourses.podbean.com[3]
- facebook.com/convocourses[4]
- Tiktok.com/@convocourses

---

1. http://convocourses.com/

2. https://www.youtube.com/c/ConvoCourses

3. http://convocourses.podbean.com/

4. http://facebook.com/convocourses

Overview of Cybersecurity Field

Some people in the industry make a distinction between information security and cybersecurity. They describe information security as focused on protecting an organization's confidentiality (secrets), integrity (authorized modifications), and availability. While cybersecurity is focused on cybercrimes, cyber fraud, law enforcement and threats on "cyber space".

By these definitions, I have done both cybersecurity and information security. And I am telling you it's a waste of time to debate the differences because there is just too much overlap. As a "cybersecurity person" you will secure information and as an information security person you must be aware of laws, cybercrimes and threats from "cyber space". Also, the US federal government and states use the terms interchangeably. The only people that want to draw a line in the sand between cybersecurity and information security are geek bloggers online who have too much time on their hands.

So in the interest of getting to the point, we will call the entire field cybersecurity and then define the categories, areas and role under one giant circus tent.

With that out of the way, let's proceed.

Cybersecurity has work that is technical, managerial, analytical, and scientific. There are some jobs that have a spectrum with some combination of each of these.

We will be using the National Initiative for Cybersecurity Education (NICE) Framework. It provides a common definition of cybersecurity, a comprehensive list of cybersecurity tasks, and the knowledge, skills, and abilities required to perform those tasks.

As comprehensive as it is, even the NICE Cybersecurity Workforce Framework misses some parts of the cybersecurity spectrum, so we will fill in the blanks with the "information security color wheel".

Information Security Color Wheel

Government, health care, financial and other organizations have adopted the term "Red Team", "Blue Team and "Purple Team" to refer to offensive and defensive security roles.

Red Team – Offensive security. These are cybersecurity professionals tasked with testing the resilience of a system or network against real attacks.

Blue Team – Defensive security. Cybersecurity professionals tasked with detecting, defending and fighting against cybersecurity attacks. Blue team tasks are covered extensively in Protect and Defend and other categories of the NICE Cybersecurity Workforce.

Purple Team – Improve the security posture. Red and Blue make purple. Purple team combines the perspective of both attackers and defenders. Individuals in this area create reports and analyze the data from offensive and defensive activities so that they can help the leadership of the organization become more secure.

Cybersecurity professional April Wright presented a more in-depth breakdown of the color schemes information security wheel at Black Hat USA 2017 cybersecurity conference that included more roles. She expanded on the cybersecurity color "team" concept, by introducing a spectrum:

Yellow Team – Software developers, system architects and engineers. These are positions tasked with building the infrastructure everyone is working on. The chapter on "Operate and Maintain" goes into these positions.

Green Team – Combination of Blue Team defense and Yellow Team builders. They enhance the security features with design and code.

Orange Team – Orange is a combination of the Red Team, who discover holes in the network, and Yellow who need to be aware of the weaknesses in the networks and systems they build. They educate and create awareness around the security vulnerabilities and risks to the organization.

White Team – These are the people tasked with coordinating the offensive and defensive activities. They will setup, document and get authorization for the penetration testing and ethical hacking that goes into the offensive Red Team activities. The White Team also documents and assesses the controls and activities of the defensive Blue Team. The NICE Cybersecurity Workforce goes into greater detail about this field of work. Their work roles include governance, risk, compliance (GRC), risk management, security control assessors, information system security managers and other compliance, management and risk analysis type positions.

April Wright (@aprilwright) is one of the cybersecurity professionals credited with the clever blending of skills using primary colors. It's a great way to explain cybersecurity roles and how they work together to protect an organization's assets.

Cybersecurity Workforce Categories

The National Institute for cybersecurity careers and study (NICCS) is managed by the Office of the Chief Learning Officer (OCLO) within the Cybersecurity and Infrastructure Security Agency (CISA).

NICCS promotes cybersecurity awareness, education, and career advancement throughout the USA. Their mission is "to be a national resource/hub for cybersecurity education, careers, and training." For more information about NICCS go to https://niccs.cisa.gov/.

NICCS created the National Initiative for Cybersecurity Education (NICE) cybersecurity workforce framework.

NICE Cybersecurity Workforce Framework gives a good breakdown of the categories of cybersecurity and the associated tasks, knowledge, and skills that are needed to perform the work.

Cybersecurity Workforce Categories

The Cybersecurity workforce has a comprehensive breakdown of cybersecurity categories, specialty areas and work roles. The categories divide up general functions important to security in information technology as a whole.

Each of these categories have areas of expertise known as "specialty areas". Within each specialty area are jobs or "work roles". The categories are a good way to understand which direction you want to go if you are interested in a cybersecurity career path.

The 7 categories breakout into over 30 specialty areas and over 50 work roles. Realistically, the work roles are limitless because they are created by each organization.

As you go through each of the specialty areas, you will notice many work roles that are not cybersecurity by themselves, but are absolutely critical to cybersecurity as a whole. For example, program management and legal advice are not specifically technical or cybersecurity positions, but without a subject matter expert in these areas, implementing effective cybersecurity is not possible in certain situations.

This is why it is important to understand that cybersecurity is not just hacking and penetration testing. An organization needs more than a firewall and use of Nmap to have comprehensive security and defense in depth to protect their assets, reputation, human resources, business and mission. Cybersecurity is in every part of the organization's structure. And you can be an active part of it.

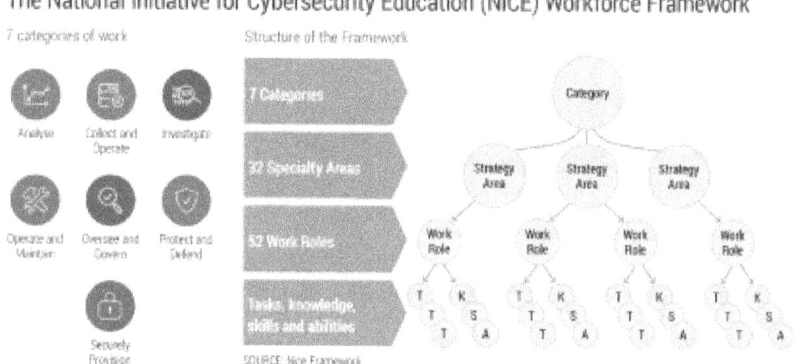

The NICE Cybersecurity workforce categories include:

⊙ **Securely Provision** – architect and design secure information systems. Securely Provision has the following specialty areas:

- Risk Management
- Software Development
- System Architecture
- System Development

- Systems Requirements Planning
- Technology R&D
- Test & Evaluation

◉ **Oversee and Govern** – manage and guide the organization so they can effectively conduct cybersecurity. The areas of expertise include:

- Cybersecurity Management
- Executive Cyber Leadership
- Legal Advice and Advocacy
- Program / Project Management and Acquisition
- Strategic Planning and Policy
- Training

◉ **Protect and Detect** – identify and analyze threats to internal information systems and networks. The specialty areas are:

- Cyber Defense Analysis
- Cyber Defense Infrastructure Support
- Incident Response
- Vulnerability Assessment and Management

◉ **Collect and Operate** – gather cybersecurity information that may be used to develop intelligence. Collect and Operate have the following specialty areas:

- Collection operations
- Cyber operational planning
- Cyber operations

◉ **Investigate** – investigate security events or crimes related to information technology. Investigate only has two specialty areas:

- Cyber investigation (cybersecurity analyst)
- Digital Forensics

◉ **Operate and Maintain** – provide support, administration and maintenance to ensure effective and efficient information systems performance and security. Operate and Maintain has these IT specialties:

- Customer services / technical support
- Data administrator
- Network services
- System administrator

◉ **Analyze** – review and evaluate incoming cybersecurity information to determine its usefulness for intelligence. The specialty areas are:

- Exploit analysis
- Threat Analysis
- Targets
- All-source analysis

These categories include management, policy, administrative technical, analytical and many other types of positions.

All US federal agencies rely on this framework. This includes the Department of Defense. The DoD created an approved baseline of certifications that is based on the Cybersecurity workforce framework (see Appendix A for more information).

We will be covering each of these categories in detail and giving insight into what the cybersecurity market wants you to do to get positions that are within these categories.

The "Analyze" Category

According to the cybersecurity workforce framework, someone within the "Analyze" category "performs highly-specialized review and evaluation of incoming cybersecurity information to determine its usefulness for intelligence."

In other words, professionals in this category review and evaluate information to figure out if the organization needs to take action.

Some real world examples of this would be a cybersecurity analyst in a security operation center (SOC). They monitor data and have to determine if the information is a security incident. They read system logs and need to determine if there is a pattern that indicates a cyberattack or the presence of malware in the environment.

Professionals in this category make anywhere from 70K USD to 120K USD annually.

The Cyber work force document lists five specialty areas:

- All-source Analysis
- Exploitation Analysis
- Language Analysis
- Targets
- Threat Analysis

All-Source Analysis

From the NICCS cyber workforce, this specialty area analyzes threat information from multiple sources, disciplines, and agencies across the Intelligence Community (IC). They gather intelligence and put it in context to gain insight about the possible implications.

Work roles under this specialty area pulls data from event logs, news feeds, and sensitive intelligence sources using applications, services and other methods. They gather all this data together to support missions and operations. These intelligence analysts are weaving together information from many sources to present a larger picture that might not be obvious at first glance.

The analyst must be able to communicate complex information, collaborate with teams, analyze large sets of data and think like a threat actor. An analyst has extensive and in-depth knowledge. They need to have a very good understanding of computer networks, cyber threats and exploitation as well as TCP/IP, virtualization and many other technologies.

When I worked at the SOC the most important skills were understanding networking (the TCP/IP three-way hand-shake), different types of hacks and exploitation of vulnerabilities and the incident response process. The very best people in this job had relevant training, certifications, experience or degrees that focused on identifying and handling security incidents. Some of the top certifications and training comes from the SANs organization. SANS has the GIAC Certified Intrusion Analyst certification (GCIA) and the GIAC Certified Incident Handler which really stand out as some of the best training you can get for this specialty area. These certifications validate a practitioner's knowledge of network and host monitoring, traffic analysis, and intrusion detection. The GCIA certification includes knowledge of advanced analysis and network forensics, concepts of TCP/IP and the Link Layer, DNS, IP Headers, Tcpdump filter and many other skills.

See *giac.org*[1] for more on analyst certifications.

The job roles include All-Source Analyst and Mission Assessment Specialist. A deeper dive on the job sites shows many other work roles including:

- Information System Security Officer
- Information Security Auditor
- Information Security Analyst
- Incident Analyst
- Cyber Analyst
- Threat Analyst
- All Source and Threat Analyst

---

1. *https://www.giac.org/*

Exploit Analysis

This specialty area analyzes information to identify vulnerabilities and potential for exploitation. Subject matter experts on Red Teams conducting offensive security fall into this area. This specialty is usually part of tasks associated with security operation centers. Work roles that conduct this task include:

- SOC Analyst
- SOC Engineer
- Cyber Security Analyst
- Cyber Security Test Engineer
- Penetration Tester
- Cyber Network Exploitation (CNE)

Tasks of exploit analysis include creating comprehensive exploitation strategies that identify exploitable technical or operational vulnerabilities. Exploit specialist sometimes require penetration testing or hacking certifications. These include but are not limited to:

- EC Council - Certified Ethical Hacker (CEH)
- EC Council - Licensed Penetration Tester (LPT)
- Infosec Institute - Certified Penetration Tester (CPT)
- Infosec Institute - Certified Expert Penetration Tester (CEPT)
- Infosec Institute - Certified Mobile and Web Application Penetration Tester (CMWAPT)
- Infosec Institute - Certified Red Team Operations Professional (CRTOP)
- CompTIA PenTest+
- Global Information Assurance Certification (GIAC) Penetration Tester (GPEN)

- GIAC - Exploit Researcher and Advanced Penetration Tester (GXPN)
- Offensive Security - Offensive Security Certified Professional (OSCP)

Although OSCP certification is among the highest levels, the government gives the most attention to CEH and GPEN exploitation certifications. The marketability changes constantly with certifications.

Language Analyst

This specialty area applies language, cultural, and technical expertise to support information collection, analysis, and other cybersecurity activities.

Work roles include Multi-Disciplined Language Analyst. These people analyze language and culture to gain more insight into information and situations. Their expertise might include interpretation of criminal activity, terrorist threats, helping to decipher messages and comments in malicious software, or translating messages on the Dark Web. They have tools like language databases to support their analysis and they specialize in specific languages. Their positions are very necessary in intelligence. If you know more than one language, this might be a specialty area for you to consider. Languages that are in demand in the USA include: Farsi, Chinese, Russian, and Korean.

If you are multilingual, this is definitely a skill you must list on your resume because you never know what organization might need you as a language specialist

Targets

This specialty area applies current knowledge of one or more regions, countries, non-state entities, and technologies. One of the job titles in this specialty area includes: "Target Developer".

A Target Developer has a group of tasks and skillsets that are critical in some security operations centers. These tasks include figuring out where criminal hackers are likely to attack. They do this by performing target system analysis and coordinating with intelligence organizations to validate which systems are being attacked or likely to be attacked. This specialty area can be part of SOC engineering or cybersecurity analysis.

Threat Analysis

Threat Analysts identify and assess the capabilities and activities of cybersecurity criminals or foreign intelligence entities. They also produce findings to help initialize or support law enforcement and counterintelligence investigations or activities.

Work roles include:

- Cybersecurity Analyst
- Cyber vulnerability specialists
- Threat Analyst
- Cybersecurity Threat Analyst
- Cyber Threat Hunter
- Computer Network Defense Analyst
- Cyber Security Incident Response

Being a Professional in the Analyst Category

The daily life of the typical analyst involves staring at a computer screen and consuming data. They work with large data sets and turn them into actionable information. Data will be in the form of individual facts, system logs, statistics, diagrams, and logs from various sources. They take all the data and turn it into reports. For example, a cyber threat hunter could analyze spreadsheets, text documents and websites with the stolen credentials from four hundred soldiers from the army. Perhaps they gathered this data from three different malicious sites on the Dark Web. After analyzing this data, they determine that there are fifteen real usernames on the list and only five of them are still active. The analyst would then create a report that explains what the actual threat was, which users and departments of the organization are affected and how this information was leaked. The analyst has to take time to gather the data, cross reference and check all the accounts, and determine where the threat came from. In this specific example, this would be a cyber threat intelligence or threat hunter type position. You can see why it would be crucial to comprehend IT well enough to be aware of potential exploits and common attacks.

(See attack.mitre.org[1] for a breakdown of the types of attacks that can occur).

The analyst would spend a lot of time searching for information, and coordinating with system administrators who have access to the affected accounts.

Many analysts do shift work in an SOC, but the nature of the work will depend on the requirements of the job. In some positions, there

---

1. https://attack.mitre.org

is a need to constantly watch audit logs and identify possible security incidents, report and respond to them in real-time.

Collect and Operate Cybersecurity Category

The "Collect and Operate" category provides specialized denial and deception operations of cybersecurity information that may be used to develop intelligence. Most of the positions in Collect and Operate are for intelligence departments working as contractors for the government. A high level clearance will be needed to allow you to access the information you will be collecting.

In the movie *Mission Impossible: Ghost Protocol*, Jeremy Renner plays a character who calls himself an "Analyst". He would have been in this category of work. In reality these jobs are not as exciting as they are depicted in the movies. Hollywood has these characters jumping off the Burj Khalifa tower in Dubai and fighting bad guys. But in reality, intelligence work is a lot of cubicles and buildings with no windows, sprinkled with some shift work where you have 40 – 50 hours a week of data analysis.

The specialty areas include:

- Collection Operations
- Cyber Operational Planning
- Cyber Operations

Collection Operations

This specialty area includes collecting intelligence from different sources for clients. The work roles, abilities, skills and tasks are for intelligence. This specialty uses different intelligence collection platforms such as systems that search for threats, databases and networks with classified intelligence data from different agencies, and information gathering tools that use artificial intelligence.

Work Roles include:

- All Source-Collection Manager
- All Source-Collection Requirements Manager

Cyber Operational Planning

This area is about Intelligence planning. The roles in this area provide support for developing, coordinating, and overseeing all aspects of the Intelligence centers activities. Work roles provide input throughout all planning functions from translating strategic guidance, through concept and plan development, to plan assessments and associated functions.

Work Roles include:

- Cyber Ops Planner
- Partner Integration Planner

Cyber Operations

Cyber operations gathers evidence on criminal or foreign intelligence entities to mitigate possible or real-time threats, protect against espionage or insider threats, and foreign sabotage and international terrorist. These are the guys in the background researching terrorist cells.

Some work roles include:

- Cyber Operator
- Cyber Analyst
- Cyberspace Intelligence Analyst
- Cyber Defense Operator

The Collect and Operate category consists of mostly intelligence jobs. Although there are degrees that specialize in this category, such as Bachelor of Science program in Cyber Operations, any degree in science, technology, engineering, or mathematics will help. Some of the non-technical Intel analyst positions will even take a degree in Intelligence Studies, Political Science, International Relations, or National Security.

For the more technical cyber analyst positions, see the same certifications that are required in the Analysis security category.

Being a Professional in the Collection and Operations Category

All of these jobs deal with intelligence. They will usually have some affiliation with the federal government. This includes the military, NSA, CIA and other organizations with a direct affiliation with national security. They will usually be operating in a building with no windows, classified phones that encrypt all messages and COMSEC (which we will talk about in another section). They do a lot of coordination with other units within the organization.

Many of these jobs do a lot of what professionals in the "Analyze" category do. There is a lot of overlap with the "All-Sources Analyst" specialty because they are spending a lot of time searching and gathering data from different sources to create reports and presentations for decision makers that need it. The main difference is that the collection and operations professional is focused on highly sensitive information in the Intelligence community.

Investigate Cybersecurity Category

This category of the cybersecurity work force focuses on investigation of crimes that involve the use of information systems, networks, and digital evidence. This part of cybersecurity has been made popular by shows like "CSI" that have cybersecurity forensics in the plot of the show from time to time. In fact, one of the spin offs of the CSI series is called *CSI: Cyber*.

The specialty areas include:

- Cyber Investigation
- Digital Forensics

Cyber Investigation

This specialty area applies tactics, techniques and procedures with a full range of investigative tools. Cyber investigation includes interviews interrogation, surveillance, and surveillance detection.

Work roles include:

- Cyber Crime Investigator
- Digital Forensics Analyst
- Criminal Investigator (Digital Forensics)

The cybercrime investigator and digital forensics specialties overlap. The primary distinction between the two is that a cybercrime investigator focuses more on law enforcement while digital forensics focuses on extracting data from information systems that are involved in crimes.

Digital Forensics

The digital forensics specialty area collects, processes, preserves, analyzes, and presents computer-related evidence in support of network vulnerability mitigation, criminal, fraud, counterintelligence, or law enforcement investigations.

The work roles include:

- Cyber Defense Forensics Analyst
- Law Enforcement / Counterintelligence Forensics Analysts
- Digital Network Exploitation Analyst

Being a Professional in the Investigate Category

The Investigate category requires a combination of experience, degrees or certifications. If you research the types of degrees for this field, you will see that many will accept any science, technical, engineering or math degree if you have experience with digital forensics. If you will be working with law enforcement, a criminal justice degree or a background in law enforcement will help.

Criminal Investigator's and digital forensics' salaries vary greatly because this skill is necessary in almost every industry. According to ZipRecruiter, the majority of digital forensics investigators make between $51K and 110K, with a national average of about $80K per year. But there are so many factors with the investigate category that it will depend on the position itself.

There are some certifications that will help get into this career field. The top certs are listed on the Department of Defense approved list. This includes the GCFA, GIAC Certified Forensic Analyst.

The training is on SANS.org[1] as *FOR508: Advanced Computer Forensic Analysis and Incident Response*. Other DoD approved certifications that are accepted for federal forensics positions include GCIA, GIAC Certified Intrusion Analyst.

There are many other forensics certifications that can help in the field:

- GIAC Certified Forensic Examiner (GCFE)
- GIAC Certified Forensic Analyst (GCFA)
- GIAC Reverse Engineering Malware (GREM)
- GIAC Network Forensic Analyst (GNFA)

---

1. https://www.sans.org/

- GIAC Advanced Smartphone Forensics (GASF)
- GIAC Cyber Threat Intelligence (GCTI)
- Computer Hacking Forensics Investigator (CHFI)
- Certified Computer Examiner (CCE)
- Cyber Security Forensic Analyst (CSFA)
- EnCase certification

Some of the tools that Digital Forensics professionals are proficient on include:

- Encase
- FTK (Forensics Toolkit)
- The Sleuth Kit
- SIFT
- Xplico
- Tcpdump
- hexadecimal dumper
- disassembler to analyze software
- debugger to analyze software
- Snort
- Zeek

Many of these positions blend in with both network forensics and cyber security analysis. Sometimes their jobs overlap or they work back-to-back in the same office on the same cases.

The daily life of a professional conducting investigative work will vary. With a focus on cybersecurity analyst work, the daily tasks will be monitoring audit logs throughout the agency. The skills of an Intrusion Analyst would come in handy for this. They spend their day doing network forensics which includes doing packet captures using tools like Wireshark, Snort, Tcpdump, SiLK and other tools. If most of their tasks include doing cyber security analyst work, they will only scan hard drives or conduct packet analysis as needed.

When I worked in a security operations center as a cybersecurity analyst, I would have to use Tcpdump and some packet capture tools. We would do a little forensics work, but as soon as it got deep, we would pass it along to our digital forensics team who would spend hours or days on a couple of potential incidents.

For the digital forensic professional working with special investigations of a law enforcement unit, they are given computer components to analyze. They use tools like FTK, EnCase and others to gather data that may be used in an ongoing criminal investigation. These computer components include internal or external hard drives, RAM, and anything that stores data. They will work with detectives, agencies and other law enforcement personnel on cases.

Positions that are heavy on digital forensics look for experience in the field above all else. Tools can be taught and certification tests can be passed, but experience conducting log file analysis is priceless.

Unspeakable Crimes

I have had two run-ins with the criminal investigations side of digital forensics work for law enforcement. Both incidents involved the same crime.

Years ago, when I was working on the Help Desk at an Air Force base, we were fixing a workstation that kept rebooting. Our attempts to remotely resolve the problem were unsuccessful, so we went to the desk of the Master Sergeant that was having the issue.

After booting it successfully in "Safe Mode" we decided that it might be malware. We ran a scan. The scan detected multiple viruses. When we looked at the drive where the malware was located, there was a whole bunch of porn. Pornography on a military system is bad. We would find it from time to time on workstations. It usually was met with a chuckle, a quick evaluation of the quality of said porn and then deletion. But there are some kinds of pornography that would get your system confiscated for further investigation with digital forensics and land the operator of that system in jail, kicked out the military and registered as a sex offender. I'm sure you can figure out what kind of pornography I'm talking about.

When we found the illegal pornography, we started a security incident that was immediately send to the Air Force Office of Special Investigations; it's the CSI of the US Air Force. They investigate domestic and international terrorists, murders and the type of porn that we found on this master sergeant's computer. The office of special investigations confiscated the system, gathered additional Internet logs from the network team and started putting all the data together to investigate the case. The last I heard of that sergeant he was in the process of losing his rank and retiring.

The second time I had a run-in with the criminal investigations side of digital forensics was when I was out of the military. I was on a small security team in an aerospace company. Once again, someone's workstation had some sort of virus on it. The system was running too slow to do work and we could not fix the issue remotely. Someone on our team had to go to the employee's office.

The cybersecurity professional ran a local scan, found the malware and a motherload of illegal pornography. The system was confiscated for further investigation. This guy was close to retirement. I don't know why someone would risk their livelihood by doing this! Especially at work. I mean, they have to know that the network is being monitored and that the organization can scan your system at any time, right?

Anyway, I digress. In digital forensics and law enforcement you really see dark stuff. Do not get into this field if you cannot handle it.

Operate and Maintain Cybersecurity Category

This category covers support, administration, and maintenance necessary to ensure effective and efficient information system performance and security. You will notice that the work roles are mostly information technology positions that include support for cybersecurity tasks rather than full time cybersecurity roles.

Specialty areas include:

- Customer Service and Technical Support
- Data Administration
- Knowledge Management
- Network Services
- System Administration
- System Analysis

Customer Service and Technical Support

Technical support specialist is a work role within the Customer Service and Technical Support specialty area. Technical customer services help customers who need endpoint support for hardware and software.

This specialty area is great for entry level positions. It also includes work roles like help desk, help desk supervisor, field technician, customer support and others.

Being in Customer Service

This work role supports the largest range of experience. What I mean is that it can accept both novices with no experience, and information technology professionals with over ten years of experience.

Since the range of professionals is so broad, the average that technical support specialist make is about $40K USD annually. Of course, there are customer service type positions that make much more than this.

Some entry level customer support positions will accept a beginner with a high school diploma or equivalent. Many companies will give on the job training, but they do expect you to come to the table with some basic IT knowledge.

As for degrees, when they do ask for a degree, they ask for everything from technical Associate's degrees to Master's degrees. It will depend on whether the system is technical, managerial or director level.

Entry level certifications that I recommend include the ones on the DoD approved list such as the CompTIA A+, Security+, ISC2 SSCP and the GSEC. But other entry level certifications that are great are Amazon AWS Cloud Practitioner and the Google IT Support Profession certification. These are marketable entry level certifications. They will not give you 100,000 USD by themselves but they are a good start.

The main tasks of customer support specialists include taking calls, requests, servicing tickets, and troubleshooting end-user devices. End-user devices includes laptops, desk top computers, and mobile devices. On a day-to-day basis they troubleshoot hardware and software issues on local systems. These tasks include doing some security on the systems such as installing security patches, updating malware signatures and ensuring that systems have proper security configurations.

Data Administration

The data administration specialty includes professionals who develop and administer databases. These data management systems allow the storage, query, protection, and utilization of data. The work roles include database administrators and data analysts.

Data Analyst

Data analysts examine data from different sources and provide insight on security and privacy. They design and implement custom algorithms for data mining and research purposes.

Database Administrator

Database administrators (also known as DBAs) have many security base tasks. These include allowing the secure storage, query, protection and utilization of data. This includes security updates and security / privacy configurations.

Being a DBA and Data Analyst

DBAs and Data analysts spend most of their time with large sets of data. The difference is that a DBA is working with the system that manages the data (the relational or object oriented databased and the hardware). They might work with Oracle, MS SQL or other vendor database systems that house the data. They might need to create queries, manage users or update security configurations on the database.

DBAs make an average of 120K USD per year and Data Analysts make an average of 90KUSD. This depends on the level of experience, location and skill set.

The top DBA certifications are:

- Oracle Certified Associate - Oracle9i Database Administrator (OCA)[1]
- Oracle Certified Professional - Oracle 9i Database Administrator (OCP)[2]
- Microsoft Certified Database Administrator (MCDBA)[3]
- Oracle 9i Database Administrator - Professional (OCP)[4]
- Oracle Database 10g Administrator Certified Professional[5]
- SQL Server 2008, Implementation and Maintenance (MCTS)[6]
- Teradata 14 Certified Master[7]

---

1. https://www.zippia.com/

2. https://www.zippia.com/

3. https://www.zippia.com/

4. https://www.zippia.com/

5. https://www.zippia.com/

6. https://www.zippia.com/

DBA positions rely heavily on experience and skills because there is a lot riding on managing the organization's databases.

A data analyst works with the organization's data. They take statistics, mean averages, sums, income, gross sales, units sold, differences and make that information into graphs, pie charts and other information that will be meaningful to the organization.

Data analyst positions vary but they are usually looking for a combination of the following skills:

- Advanced Microsoft Excel skills
- Pivot Tables, Macros
- Strong communication skills, both written and verbal
- Experience working with Big Data
- Structured Query Language (SQL)
- Machine learning algorithms
- Data visualization/Tableau
- Python and other scripting languages
- Decision-making
- Building data sets
- Machine learning models
- Predictive modeling
- Statistical analysis
- Data engineering
- Regression analysis
- Data optimization

Some of the tools that data analysts use include:

- Microsoft Excel
- Python

- "R" analytics
- Jupyter Notebook (jupyter.org)
- Apache Spark
- SAS
- Microsoft Power B.I.
- Tableau
- KNIME

Data analytics positions are not usually looking for any particular IT certifications. But here are a few of the top data analyst certifications:

- CompTIA Data+
- Microsoft Certified Data Analyst Associate
- Cloudera Certified Associate (CCA) Data Analyst
- SAS Certified Big Data Professional
- Certified Analytics Professional (CAP)
- Amazon AWS Certified Data Analytics
- IBM Data Science Professional Certificate
- Google Data Analytics Professional Certificate

Knowledge Management

The Knowledge Manager position is under the knowledge management specialty, and this person is responsible for administering tools that allow an organization to identify, document, and access its content.

The Knowledge Manager Role

Knowledge manager positions vary in responsibilities based on the industry. In the government, the knowledge manager may need to coordinate with servicemen, civil servants and contractors to develop training and knowledge transfer requirements and policies. A military or Intelligence based knowledge manager may help protect and distribute classified information in the correct way.

In a more technical role, the knowledge manager will be more like DBAs where they provide analysis, design, development, and deployment support for customer database requirements. They may need to know SQL and how to create queries.

The degrees and experience level also vary greatly based on the job and the organization's data requirements.

I have seen organizations take program managers, information system security officers or general managers and make them the official knowledge manager.

Network Services

The Cybersecurity Workforce only mentions the network operator specialist as a work role. A network operator specialist "plans, implements, and operates network services, to include hardware and virtual environments". The full breakdown of network services in the NICE framework is a little out of touch. So, we will address what you really need to know about this specialty area.

First of all, I seldom ever come across the job titles "network operator specialist" in network services. Network engineers and network administrators is what we call them in the IT industry. You have network technicians, network support, and other names but the most popular are engineers and administrators. There are basic skills all network operators need to know for network switches and routers and other internetworking devices. They need to know how to setup a local area network, connect to a wide area network, configure, upgrade, and backup a switch, router or other internetworking devices.

There are different specialties in network operations. Voice over IP (VOIP), network security, virtual networks and others. Network support only does work when something breaks or if there is a change needed on the network. Network operators have these types of skills:

- Network engineering
  - LAN management
  - WAN management
- Operational support
- OSI model
- Multicasting knowledge: IPv4 and IPv6
- Virtual networking

Being an Entry-Level Network Associate

The network industry is dominated by a few huge organizations that have a bit of an oligopoly on the IT market. As such, if you are a network engineer you will need to eventually know at least one vendor's products and services well.

The major companies providing professional network enterprise services are:

- Cisco
- Juniper Networks
- NVIDIA
- VMware
- Hewlett Packard Enterprise (Aruba Networks)
- Riverbed Technology
- Extreme Networks
- NetScout

The organizations that have the best products and services for an IT professional to know are Cisco, VMware and Juniper.

Unfortunately, because their products and services are continuously changing, their certificates also do. The following breakdown of vendor certifications may have changed by the time you read this.

For Cisco, the entry level certification is called CCT (Cisco Certified Technician). At the time of this writing, it is the only entry-level Cisco cert below the CCNA (Cisco Certified Network Associate) which is an intermediate certification.

Another Entry level network certification is the CompTIA Network+. Although not many organizations are looking for this certification, it will give you a good idea of the basics of networks.

Juniper Networks Certified Associate, or Junos (JNCIA-Junos), is the associate-level certification for Juniper Networks technologies. It covers the fundamentals of networking using Juniper systems.

VMware's certification path starts with the VMware Certified Technical Associate (VCTA). This certification is for entry-level operators new to the industry of virtualized environments.

Each of the industry leaders in network enterprise solutions have their own training and certifications. The entry level certifications don't have as much marketability but they are great for learning and getting your foot in the door.

Intermediate network engineers

The intermediate networking level is where the money is made. These are certifications that are highly sought after by many employers around the world. These include:

- Cisco Certified Network Associate (CCNA)
- Juniper Networks enterprise routing and switching platforms (JNCIS-ENT)
- VMware Certified Professional

The job of an intermediate network engineer is to install, configure, and troubleshoot networks using products from one of the major networking service providers. The intermediate certification will allow an associate to work as a technician in one or more areas, including routing and switching, security, wireless services, or data center operations. While specifics of the job vary, the responsibilities may involve evaluating network performance, defining policies and procedures, and improving network security. Some of the necessary skills include:

- Network engineering

- Routing protocols: EIGRP, OSPF, BGP
- Operational support
- SAN networking knowledge
- Unified Communication
- OSI model
- Multicasting knowledge: IPv4 and IPv6
- Firewalls
- Virtual networking

Professional Level Network Engineers

A network engineer at the professional level is responsible for maintaining, implementing, and resolving technical issues relating to local and wide area networks at the enterprise level using the applicable network device. They have the skills to collaborate with specialists in cybersecurity, Voice over IP, wireless, and video solutions. The need to be able to activate and manage routing protocols such as EIGRP and OSPF that are necessary for getting wide area networks to communicate.

Network professionals can design and develop Layer 3 Path Control Solutions and broadband connections as well as VLAN based solutions for an enterprise. The certifications include (but are not limited to):

- Cisco Certified Network Professional (CCNP)
- VMware Certified Professional (VCP)
- Enterprise Routing and Switching, Professional (JNCIP-ENT)

Systems Administrator

System Admins are the first work role that come to mind when people think about "operate and maintain". There are system admins for every type of system from desktops to servers to firewalls.

Excluding network and database administrators, most system admins are either Red Hat or Microsoft professionals. Truthfully, the term "system administrator" can cover just about anything from firewalls to mainframes to web servers. Regardless of the technology, they are doing operational management of the system.

These days, most companies require certifications of their system administrators to ensure that their employees are not falling behind. There are exceptions. Some organizations don't care about certifications or degrees, but in these cases, they lean heavily on proven skills and knowledge level. According to the US Bureau of Labor Statistics, systems administrator roles are projected to grow 4 percent from 2019 to 2029.

Here are some common requirements that you would find in a system administrator job description:

- Install and configure software, hardware and networks
- Ensure security and efficiency of IT infrastructure
- Monitor system performance and troubleshoot issues
- Identify system requirements and install upgrades
- Maintains, secure and upgrade a web system
- Create a backup and safeguard the data
- Perform account setup for new and old employees
- Track emerging technologies and implement them in the organization

Some of the most marketable certifications include:

- Microsoft Certified Solutions Expert (MCSE)
- VMware Certified Professional (VCP)
- Oracle Linux System Administrator (Oracle)
- ITIL® Certification[1]
- Red Hat Certified Engineer (RHCE)

This list changes with the trends of the market.

---

1. https://www.simplilearn.com/it-service-management/itil-foundation-training

Oversee and Govern Cybersecurity Category

This category provides leadership, management, guidance and advocacy so the organization may effectively conduct cybersecurity work. This is one of the most important categories that doesn't get the attention it deserves. It includes security compliance, governance, C-Level executives, program management and training.

The specialty areas include:

- Cybersecurity Management
- Executive Cyber Leadership
- Legal Advice and Advocacy
- Program/Project Management and Acquisition
- Strategic Planning and Policy
- Training, Education, and Awareness

Cybersecurity Management

Cybersecurity management is a specialty area that oversees the cybersecurity program of an information system or network. This category focuses on managing the risks that an information system has and how it will impact the organization as a whole. This includes strategic, personnel, infrastructure, requirements, policy enforcement, and resources.

Work roles mentioned in the cybersecurity workforce framework include:

- Communications Security (COMSEC) Manager
- Information System Security Manager (ISSM)

Communications Security (COMSEC)

The COMSEC officer is the key custodian of Crypto Keys. This is sometimes known as a Crypto Key Management System (CKMS). A COMSEC officer needs to have knowledge of computers and networking concepts such as network security methods. They need to have some understanding of the laws and security policies that govern the COMSEC process as well as knowledge of cryptography. COMSEC is done by other security positions such as Facility Security Officers and Information Systems and Security Manager (ISSM).

If you research the work roles in the market, you will see this job given to Information System Security Officers, Program Security Officers, Contract Special Security Officers (CSSO), Contract Special Security Officers, and System Security Engineer positions. These are highly classified jobs working with military departments and the Intelligence Community.

Employers of COMSEC officers are looking for Active Top Secret clearances. They are looking for someone who has experience interpreting and enforcing government and company security policies, and providing direction.

Information System Security Manager (ISSM)

An ISSM is responsible for cybersecurity of a program, organization, system or enclaves. The ISSM manages the Information System Security Officer (ISSO). Information system security covers part of governance, risk and compliance (GRC), because their main focus is on security compliance. All major industries have to comply with governing country, state and industry rules and regulations.

For example, in the USA, the healthcare industry must comply with Health Insurance Portability and Accountability Act of 1996 (HIPAA). The financial industry must follow the rules of the Sarbanes Oxley Act (SOX). SOX requires all financial reports to include an Internal Controls Report. The US government requires all federal information systems to abide by the Federal Information Security Modernization Act (FISMA) which has NIST special publication 800 guidance. Each industry in each country and state has different rules and regulations they must abide by and the ISSM is a role that assists with this.

Being an Information System Security Professional Jobs

ISSM specifically is a management role over information system security professionals. Information System Security professionals cover a large part of security compliance. There is a wide range of job titles for them in the US federal government:

- Compliance officers
- Risk Compliance
- Information System Security Officers
- Cyber Security Engineer
- Senior Information System Security Officer

In the healthcare industry they have a different set of titles:

- Compliance Analyst
- Privacy Compliance
- Risk Analyst Health Information
- IS Security GRC Analyst
- Chief Compliance Officer
- Senior Cybersecurity Risk Analyst
- Compliance officer

In the financial sector, the names are as follows:

- Cybersecurity Senior Analyst
- Information Security Risk and Compliance Analyst
- Senior Analyst, Internal Controls – IT SOX
- SOX Consultant
- Information Security Governance Analyst

Regardless of the industry, what all these information system security positions and titles have in common is that they all focus on managing the organization's adherence to the industry compliance and help to manage the organization's risk.

Government information security positions lean heavily toward years of experience in IT, but that experience can be leveraged with a degree in STEM (science, technology, engineering or mathematics) or a relevant IT certification.

A CISSP, Security+ or security certification, a BS degree and some IT experience are excellent qualifications for employment in this field with the government doing compliance. But this varies from place to place so make sure you check the requirements of the organization. A solid understanding of ISO 27000, GDPR, NIST, IEC62443 or any security compliance framework is a great way to get in.

A good way to learn more about GRC work is to pursue certifications that focus on this.

ISC2 Certified Governance, Risk and Compliance (CGRC) – This certification is formerly known as the Certified Authorization Professional (CAP). The CGRC focuses on the US federal security compliance which comes from the Federal Information Security Modernization Act of 2014 and other federal regulations. These federal laws promote the need for security controls, assessments, continuous monitoring and risk management framework. The guidance for this process is in National Institute of Standards and Technology special publications, NIST 800-37, 800-30, 800-53, FIPS 200 and other documents. The domains of the CGRC are information security risk management program, the scope of the information system, selection and approval of security and privacy controls and implementation of security and privacy controls.

ISCA Certified Information Systems Auditor (CISA) - CISA certification for those who audit, control, monitor and assess an organization's information technology and business systems. If you are an entry-level to mid-career professional, CISA can showcase your expertise and assert your ability to apply a risk-based approach to planning, executing and reporting on audit engagements.

ISACA Certified in Risk and Information Systems Control (CRISC) - CRISC focuses on enterprise IT risk management. The domains of this certification are governance, IT risk assessment, risk response and reporting, and IT and security.

ISACA Certified in the Governance of Enterprise IT (CGEIT) – The CGEIT is agnostic. It does not focus on any one framework. This certification covers handling the governance of an entire organization. The domains consist of governance of enterprise IT, IT resources, befits realization and risk optimization.

There are other GRC certifications, but these are the ones with the most marketability at the time of this writing.

Executive Cyber Leadership

These are C-Level executive positions that perform cyber security functions. Examples would be director and chief positions such as chief information officer, chief security officer and others. They are leaders that make decisions that affect the overall direction of the organization and how resources are allocated.

C-Level executives usually hold a master's degree in their trade with a decade or more of experience. I used to think that all C-Level execs were privileged political types that just knew the right people to be given that position... I was wrong.

If you take a look at an executive or director's resume you will usually find something out of the ordinary in their past. They ran (or created) successful organizations, they were brilliant at a prestigious university, they were a high-level officer in the military, they worked at the organization for 20+ years or they started at a low position and climbed the corporate ladder. There will usually be something exceptional about them regardless of any advantages they might have had to get their position.

Chief Information Security Officers

Chief Information Security Officers and Directors of Security tend to be very talented technical experts. In my experience they usually have an incredible depth of technical knowledge on more than one thing. They will sometimes have some combination of a ridiculous number of certifications, a long history in IT, or a graduate degree. The most impressive executives specializing is security are also good at leading.

Once you get to this level, you will need to have your technical skills take a back seat because your job is to lead, provide resources and push the organization to the next level.

Legal Advice and Advocacy

As information processing, storage and transmission has become the center piece of our lives, it makes sense that the legal ramifications of that information must be considered. This specialty provides legal guidance on policy that the organizations sets forth. Work roles include:

- Cyber Legal Advisor
- Privacy Officer / Privacy Compliance Manager

Cyber Legal Advisor

This work role provides legal advice and recommendations on cyber law. Some other related titles include Cyber Claim Counsel, legal counsel, compliance counsel, cyber security associate, and cyber / data / privacy attorney.

The path of this work role requires legal experience. Often, cyber legal advisors are lawyers or paralegals. The cyber legal advisor is expected to have knowledge of data breaches and privacy laws (HIPAA, GLBA, FERPA, CCPA, GDPR, etc.). For cyber claim counsels, the expectation is that there is experience with handling claims.

Responsibilities might include:

- Incident response for cybersecurity and data privacy incidents
- Analysis of state, federal, and international privacy laws
- Drafting legal notices of a data breach to individuals and regulators
- Responding to regulatory investigations arising out of a data breach
- Defending privacy lawsuits

- Drafting privacy and security policies and procedures pursuant to HIPAA, GLBA, CCPA, and other statutes

Certifications that might help this position:

- Certified Paralegal (CP) or Certified Legal Assistant (CLA)
- CORE Registered Paralegal (CRP) or PACE Registered Paralegal (RP)
- American Alliance Certified Paralegal (AACP)
- Advanced Paralegal Certification (APC)
- Professional Paralegal (PP)

Other relevant requirements that you will see for this position includes (but is not limited to):

- A Bachelor's Degree
- Properly licensed, registered or authorized, and in good standing to practice law in the jurisdiction in which you will be working
- Multiple years of relevant legal experience
- J.D. (Juris Doctorate Degree) from an ABA accredited law school
- Licensed or eligible to practice in the applicable state
- Ability to effectively communicate, both written and oral, with the intended audience
- Ability to exercise sound judgment in a fast-paced environment
- Ability to exercise agility and adaptability in providing legal advice

Privacy Officer / Privacy Compliance Manager

Privacy Officers oversee privacy compliance programs of the organization. They are available to provide expertise on governance and policy as well as incident response where privacy is a factor. They might conduct privacy assessments or create privacy documents.

Some other names of this position are:

- Compliance Officer
- Risk and Privacy Officer
- Cybersecurity Officer
- Data Privacy Officer
- Data Privacy specialist
- Privacy - Legal and Compliance Specialist
- Privacy Specialist

Certifications that might help a privacy officer:

- **CIPP** [1]**(Certified Information Privacy Professional)** - This certification applies to both the U.S. (CIPP/US) and Europe (CIPP/E) law and regulation.
- **CIPM**[2] **(Certified Information Privacy Manager** - The CIPM covers implementing privacy in an organization.
- **CIPT**[3] **(Certified Information Privacy Technologist)** - It covers implementing privacy in applications and systems.

---

1. https://www.infosecinstitute.com/courses/cipp-us-certification-training-boot-camp/?utm_source=resources&utm_medium=infosec%20network&utm_campaign=cour se%20pricing&utm_content=hyperlink

2. https://www.infosecinstitute.com/courses/cipm-certification-training-boot-camp/?utm_source=resources&utm_medium=infosec%20network&utm_campaign=cour se%20pricing&utm_content=hyperlink

3. https://www.infosecinstitute.com/courses/cipt-certification-training-boot-camp/?utm_source=resources&utm_medium=infosec%20network&utm_campaign=cour se%20pricing&utm_content=hyperlink

- **CDPSE[4] (Certified Data Privacy Solutions Engineer)** - CDPSE is for IT professionals who work with technology and then store, collect and transport personally identifiable information.

---

4. https://www.infosecinstitute.com/courses/certified-data-and-privacy-solutions-engineer-cdpse-boot-

camp/?utm_source=resources&utm_medium=infosec%20network&utm_campaign=course%20pricing&utm_content=hyperlink

Program/Project Management and Acquisition

Applies knowledge of data, information, processes, organizational interactions, skills, and analytical expertise, as well as systems, networks, and information exchange capabilities to manage acquisition programs. Executes duties governing hardware, software, and information system acquisition programs and other program management policies. Provides direct support for acquisitions that use information technology (IT) (including National Security Systems), applying IT-related laws and policies, and provides IT-related guidance throughout the total acquisition life cycle.

IT Investment / Portfolio Manager

This position manages a portfolio of IT investments that align with the overall mission and enterprise priorities. Portfolio managers are investment decision-makers. They construct and manage portfolios, choose what and when to acquire and sell investments, and devise and implement investment strategies and processes to suit client goals and constraints.

Program managers / Project Managers

Here is a little more about program and project management as a work role. Project managers are a crucial part of medium and large system and software engineering projects. They provide scheduling for the development of old and new systems.

If you don't want to be technical, project management is one of the best career paths you could do because there are a lot of positions for this that are aligned closely with cybersecurity, science, software and engineering projects. Many of these positions have remuneration that are comparable to their technical counterparts.

Project Management Professional (PMP)

This means skilled project managers are in high demand. The PMP certification is designed by project professionals, for project professionals and validates that you are among the best—highly skilled in:

- **People:** emphasizing the soft skills you need to effectively lead a project team in today's changing environment.
- **Process:** reinforcing the technical aspects of successfully managing projects.
- **Business Environment:** highlighting the connection

between projects and organizational strategy.

PMP certification validates that you have the project leadership skills employers seek. The new PMP includes three key approaches:

- **Predictive** (waterfall)
- **Agile**
- **Hybrid**

Protect & Detect Cybersecurity Category

This category is for all cybersecurity professionals who identify, analyze and mitigate threats to internal information systems and networks. There is some overlap with the Analyze, Investigate and Operate, and Maintain categories because Protecting and Detecting requires skills from each one of these. The difference is that this category is taking action to do something about the threats.

Protect & Detect includes the following specialty areas:

- Cyber Defense Analysis
- Cyber Defense Infrastructure Support
- Incident Response
- Vulnerability Assessment and Management

Cyber Defense Analysis

According to the Cybersecurity and Infrastructure Security Agency (CISA), cyber defense analysis, "Uses defensive measures and information collected from a variety of sources to identify, analyze, and report events that occur or might occur within the network to protect information, information systems, and networks from threats."

The work role that cisa.gov mentions is "Cyber Defense Analyst", but in the cybersecurity field there are many titles for this role. There is information security analyst, cybersecurity analyst, cybersecurity vulnerability analyst and many others. There is even a position in the National Security Agency for this role called "Forensic Analyst". The role title sounds more like it should be a part of the "Investigate" category. But don't get too wrapped up in the titles of the roles. Since the organization determines what the tasks, knowledge base and title of the role is, the names of the positions will vary. But the work consists of using data collected from intrusion detection systems, firewalls, network traffic logs and other cyber defense tools to mitigate risk.

There is a lot of overlap between this work role and the Analyst cybersecurity category, but the difference is that cyber defense collects this information to actively fix the problem.

When I was doing cybersecurity analyst work for the DoD, I can tell you that there is really not that much difference because the organization might have you shutting down ports with an intrusion prevention one day and doing nothing but analyzing network traffic the next.

Cyber Defense Infrastructure Support

Cyber defense infrastructure support is closely related to cyber defense analyst. The difference is that they focus on making sure that the analyst has the tools to do their job effectively.

When I was in the SOC working with the DoD, I transferred from doing analyst work monitoring the traffic in shifts and correlating data using a security information event manager (SIEM) to supporting the SIEM. I was installing new SIEM hardware, creating reports, queries and dashboards for the cyber analysts.

The work tempo and mindset changed because I went from an all-seeing eye of the network—always watching the network in shifts with my fellow analysts—to someone in more of an "operate and maintain" stance. We would respond if something was broken and we'd be working to update patches but this did not have to be done in a shift.

For Cyber Defense Infrastructure, you will need to know the hardware, software and configurations of the cybersecurity tools.

Being a Cyber Defense Analyst

The government and contracting organizations look for a combination of STEM BS degrees, cybersecurity experience, and cybersecurity certifications. It is also important to have a good understanding of incident response.

Incident Response

An "incident" refers to something that will damage the organization, the asset, the data or the flow of data on a system. These can be malware, a hack, a leak or a mishap. As a cybersecurity analyst, we were part of the incident response team. As such, we were part of the incident response process. This process takes on a few different shapes but we will address the 6-step process that is used by the US government:

1. Preparation: plan ahead before a security incident.
2. Identification: detect and determine what kind of incident (if any).
3. Containment: limit the impact of the incident.
4. Eradication: remove the threat causing the incident.
5. Recovery: restore the affected system or information.
6. Lessons Learned: investigate the root cause.

As cyber defense analysts, we were mostly part of the identification, containment and eradication section of the incident response team. There were incident handlers whose main job was to follow the organization's response from preparation to lessons learned throughout the entire process. There are many names for professional incident handlers:

- Incident Response Analysts
- Technical Security Investigators

- Incident Commander
- Incident Responder
- Incident Response Lead

The names of the positions are irrelevant because there are many positions that will have a hand in incident response tasks. So, their title might be Information Security Associate, Digital Forensics Incident Responder, Security Engineer, Cybersecurity Analyst, Information System Security Officer, or whatever.

Vulnerability Assessment and Management

Vulnerability management is important within an organization's security process. Vulnerabilities are constantly being discovered on all operating systems, applications, hardware, and firmware. Sometimes the vendor catches them and announces a patch or configuration that must be implemented to remediate the risk. And sometimes hackers discover weaknesses in the system. The organization must be proactive in conducting regular vulnerability assessments to have strong cyber defenses. The workload is so heavy in medium and large environments that companies and government departments usually have an office dedicated solely to vulnerability management.

Tips on Cyber Defense Analysis Positions

All Cyber Defense Analysis positions have the same types of certifications that employers like to see. The top paying cybersecurity certifications that are marketable for this field are:

- CISSP
- CISA
- CEH
- GCIA
- GCIH
- Security+
- CYSA+
- GPEN

There are others but these will be the most popular because they are listed on the DoD approved certification list. These are listed in Appendix A under Cybersecurity Service Provider Analyst and Cybersecurity Services Provider Infrastructure Support and Cybersecurity Services Provider Incident Handler.

Securely Provision Cybersecurity Category

This category provides concepts, designs, procedures and building secure information systems and networks. The focus is on making sure that security controls are being put in place as systems are being developed.

The specialty areas are:

- Risk Management
- Software Development
- System Architecture
- System Development
- Systems Requirements Planning
- Technology R&D
- Test and Evaluation

Risk Management

This specialty area is responsible for overseeing, evaluating and supporting the documentation, validation, assessment and authorization process required to ensure that new and existing systems meet risk requirements.

The Information System Security Manager (ISSM) and team will do a lot of the documentation and assist with assessments for the authorization process, but this specialty is focused on overseeing the final product. This is done by the Authorizing Official and the Security Control Assessor roles.

Authorizing Official / Designating Representative

These are upper-level managers, senior officials, C-Level executives or high-level officers. The organization gives them authority to formally assume responsibility for the secure operations of an information system at an acceptable level of risk.

The reason why this position is important is that having a high-level person sign on behalf of the organization ensures that there will be a serious level of scrutiny when considering the protection of the organization's assets, individuals and even the nation. CIO, CISOs, commanders, and directors are often tasked with being the Authorizing Official for a given system. In my experience, the AO is more of a duty than a permanent position.

Security Control Assessor (SCA)

SCAs conduct comprehensive assessments of all the security controls implemented on a system. This includes the technical, management, operational, physical and environmental controls of an information system. Organizations depend on SCA's to conduct independent, impartial assessments to determine if the controls have been implemented effectively. The SCA gathers the requirements of the organization. They create a security assessment plan that specifies what will be assessed, the scope of the assessment, who will be needed as a point of contact, the timing, and the location of the assessment. When they conduct the assessment, they conduct interviews, test security components and observe the security features and documentation. The results of the assessment are put into a security assessment report and delivered to the leadership of the organization.

Since SCA teams need all types of skillsets, the experience levels and certifications will vary. The tools and techniques they use might include:

- Network / vulnerability scanners
- Compliance scanners
- Code analysis tools
- Web scanners
- Policy, process and procedures reviews
- Wireless assessments
- Penetration testing
- Phishing campaign
- Social Engineering
- Physical security checks
- Cloud security assessment

All of this depends on the organization's requirements and the type of assessment being conducted.

Software Development

Software development must include methods to secure the code being developed. Software developers should follow a software development life cycle (SDLC). Software development life cycle is a process of planning, Analysis, Design, Implementation, Testing and Integration and Maintenance. The SDLC creates, tests and deploys information systems across hardware and software. During the SDLC process the organization is supposed to have security in mind from the beginning of the process. A project manager is a huge help in the software development process.

There are various SDLC methods including:

Waterfall – a linear model that has the software development go in steps. The next step cannot start until the last one is complete.

Agile – this process relies on user input and experience from the old application, to make the new software better. This allows more responsive feedback for better software releases.

Iterative – a process that focuses on baby steps. Making small improvements where needed on the software.

DevOps – similar to Agile, it focuses on usability, gathering user feedback and making improvements. This is done during design and implementation phases.

Spiral – uses a combination of iterative SDLC method and sequential to allow incremental release of software.

Cybersecurity workforce points out two work roles in the software development specialty area: Secure Software Assessor and Software Developer.

Software Engineers

Security is very important in software engineering even though it is sometimes regarded as an afterthought.

Currently, the most in-demand programming languages are JavaScript, Python, HTML, CSS, Java, SQL, NoSQL, C#, Rust, Perl, Go, PHP.

1. JavaScript

JavaScript is responsible for making the websites you go to more responsive. When you hover over a menu it seems to pop off the pages or change colors. This is usually JavaScript code making this happen. Some of what you see in search engines, social media, phone apps and ecommerce is not possible without JavaScript. It is currently the most used client-side scripting language. Things like autocomplete, validation of web form input, loading content to a page without reloading the page, animated page elements and many other things are possible because of JavaScript.

What this language is usually used for:

- Web development
- Game development
- Mobile apps
- Building web servers

2. Python

Python is one of the top languages for cybersecurity professionals to use. It can automate tasks across the cyberattack life cycle for both cyber attackers and defenders. It's used for malware analysis, decoding packets, network scans, server access and much more. Data scientists also use it for visualizing data.

What this language is used for:

- Backend development
- Automating tasks
- Data science
- App development

3. HTML

Hypertext Markup Language is the language that needs no introduction. It is used for website development, web documents, and website maintenance.

4. CSS

Cascading Style Sheets (CSS) is a style sheet language used for describing the presentation of a document written in a markup language such as HTML.

5. Java

Java is a class-based, object-oriented programming language that is designed to have as few implementation dependencies as possible. As such, it is used for just about everything. It can be used to make applications for almost every platform from supercomputers to web sites. It is used in every industry.

6. SQL

Structured Query Language is a language for databases. It is used to communicate with databases in order to manage, sort and filter data. SQL is commonly used for:

- Database management
- Sales reports
- Business management

7. NoSQL

Unlike Structured Query Language, NoSQL is used for different database management models besides traditional relational databases including document, columnar and graph formats.

8. C# / C++

C# and C++ are programming languages that are used for operating systems, applications, games, data structure and many other things. These languages are commonly used in:

- Game development
- Desktop/web/mobile apps
- VR

9. Rust

Rust is a low-level programming language. This means that it is used to communicate directly with hardware and memory. It is used for:

- Operating systems
- VR
- Web browsers

10. Perl

Like Python, Perl is often used for backend server automation. It is used by system administrators for network programming and graphic user interface development. It is a great language to learn for cybersecurity professionals to process log files or grab data.

11. Go

Go is a language that is used for system and network programming, audio/video editing, and Big Data.

12. PHP

PHP is used for server side scripting, managing dynamic content, and is compatible with all operating systems.

Regardless of the language, software needs to be developed with security in mind.

Secure Software Assessor

The work role Secure Software Assessor has many different names including Security Control Assessor, Application Security Engineer (AppSec), Cyber Security Third Party Assessor, and Information Security Risk Assessment Analyst.

Their job is to analyze the security of new or existing computer applications, software, or specialized utility programs, and provide actionable results.

Secure Software Assessors are expected to have an understanding of security best practices and experience with one or more programming languages. A deep understanding of cybersecurity frameworks and standards will sometimes be expected with certain organizations. Cybersecurity frameworks and laws include: PCI, HIPAA, Data Privacy, NIST 800, or ISO 27001/27002.

Some employers are looking for experience in software analysis tools that provide Static Application Security Testing (SAST), Dynamic Analysis Security Testing (DAST), Software Composition Analysis (SCA), Interactive Application Security Test (IAST), Runtime Application Self Protection (RASP), and threat modeling.

System Architecture

If you look up a system architect you will find position titles like Cybersecurity Engineer, System Security Engineer and many others. The System Architecture specialist area is about developing and maintaining business, system, and information processes to support enterprise mission needs. This specialty also develops information technology rules and requirements that describe baseline and target architectures.

Enterprise and Security Architects

Information Technology security architects ensure that all individuals involved with the development of the system follow the rules and requirements that describe the baseline.

The Enterprise Architects supports the design and implementation of the system's architecture. They are part of the development effort. They provide technical expertise in creating, updating, and maintaining architecture data as related to the organization's architectural framework.

The Enterprise Architecture will have deep understanding of technical architectures, putting networks and information systems together. They might have a background in implementing solutions in a cloud environment and making it compliant with NIST security or other security frameworks.

Security Architects ensure that the stakeholder security requirements necessary to protect the organization's mission and business process are in place.

System Development

The System Development Specialty Area focuses on the development phases of the systems development life cycle. It is important that the security features are considered during the system development life cycle (SDLC) of a system. Many organizations will attempt to put security into a system after it is already in production. This is both risky and expensive. It is risky because they don't know the potential weaknesses exposed in a production environment where the system is storing, processing or transferring mission essential data. It is expensive because it is much harder to put the security features in after it has already been designed, installed or implemented.

The System Development Specialty Area has two work roles that develop the system: Information Systems Security Developer & Systems Developer. Adhering to the SDLC is a normal part of any cybersecurity job that involves the development of the system.

Systems Requirements Planning

The Systems Requirements Planning consults with customers to gather and evaluate functional requirements and translates them into technical solutions. In some cases, they assist with development and maintenance of the program protection plan & cybersecurity strategy.

Every time I have encountered them, they have represented the organization and worked with the program manager and other subject matter experts to make sure the system requirements are being met.

DoD Approved Baseline Certifications has a focus on system security architecture. These are listed under the Information Assurance System Architect and Engineer (IASAE). The suggested certifications include:

- CompTIA CASP+ CE

- ISC2 CISSP (or Associate)
- ISC2 CSSLP
- ISC2 CISSP-ISSAP
- ISC2 CISSP-ISSEP
- ISC2 CCSP

Technology and Testing

The last two Specialty Areas of the Securely Provision category are Technology R&D and Test and Evaluate. Technology R&D is for research and Development. R&D conducts technology assessments and integration processes. They support prototypes in testing environments and evaluate their utility.

Test and Evaluations, sometimes called T&E, develop tests to evaluate compliance with organizational requirements. They also conduct the tests. They verify and validate whether the system is functional for operators and performs satisfactorily.

I have worked closely with T&E as a cybersecurity professional. We would have a new mission critical system that was a prototype. I was there to make sure that the security controls were in place and the verification and validation team (T&E) was there to make sure the system worked properly. We called this team verification and validation, but their official title was Systems Engineering. Their main job was to ensure that all government requirements were met on the system. They had comprehensive technical drawings of every single component of the system. They had technical writers, requirements people and a manager.

Most of the requirements people had BS or MS degrees in STEM, a technical background in either computers or engineering, and had to know a lot about how the system's main components worked.

Cybersecurity Scientists & Mathematicians

I have worked for a couple of agencies that had scientists. Many times they would have issues with applying security controls. Sometimes they needed special systems with custom security features. Some security controls would make their job harder or interfere with their research. They didn't understand why any security features needed to be implemented if they were the only person touching the system.

With all the recent leaks of sensitive information and multimillion dollar breaches, everyone has a better understanding of why cybersecurity is so important.

Engineers, analysts and technicians get a lot of the spotlight. These work roles are all over the Cybersecurity Workforce Framework. But you won't find too many scientists and mathematicians covered in the framework.

These two areas are foundational to a lot of the most important work currently being done in cybersecurity. Compilers and programming languages, cryptography, networking protocols, and central processing units (just to name a few) are based on mathematics and science.

Cybersecurity Scientist

Engineers and scientists are often used interchangeably but the two roles have different goals. A scientist in IT is usually discovering, analyzing, testing or developing something new that is not yet intended for commercial use. Engineers in IT are often working with commercial components to develop, analyze, or fix a solution that is within the requirements of an organization. Despite certain similarities, there are many differences between them. Engineers work on practical, operational systems that are already in production, whereas scientists frequently work in a lab on theoretical systems that may never make it to a real-world environment.

Scientists will have doctorates and master's degrees and be very deep in one area or another. At this level, IT certifications are irrelevant because their level of knowledge and degrees have eclipsed any certification they might have. But there are exceptions.

Here are some examples of actual job titles that a cybersecurity scientist might have:

- Research Analysts & Post Doctorate
- Cyber-crime scientist
- Data Scientist - Cybersecurity
- Research Scientist
- Laboratory Scientist
- Research Data Scientist
- Computational Scientist
- Cybersecurity Data Scientist
- Cybersecurity Computer Scientist
- Threat Data Scientist
- Professor

Cryptographers / Mathematicians

I used to think that most mathematicians worked as teachers or professors at a university writing on large chalkboards. I didn't see much practical use for advanced mathematics in everyday life. I was wrong.

Many people are familiar with mathematicians in academia, but mathematicians also work in many other fields, including:

- Astronomy and space exploration
- Climate study
- Medicine
- National security
- Robotics
- Animated films

According to the Department of Labor, the top employers of mathematicians and statisticians are the federal government, and scientific research and development companies. Mathematicians and statisticians may work on teams with engineers, scientists, and other specialists.

Mathematicians held about 2,000 jobs in 2021. The largest employers of mathematicians were as follows:

Federal government – 62%

Professional, scientific, and technical services – 13%

Colleges, universities, and professional schools; state, local, and private – 13%

Statisticians held about 34,200 jobs in 2021. The largest employers of statisticians were as follows:

Federal government – 15%

Research and development in the physical, engineering, and life sciences – 14%

Colleges, universities, and professional schools; state, local, and private – 9%

Healthcare and social assistance – 8%

Insurance carriers and related activities – 6%

Many of the mathematicians working in the federal government are doing cryptography. Cryptography is the study of secure communication techniques that allow only the sender and intended recipient of a message to view its contents.

Within government agencies like the FBI and NSA, there are self-contained training programs for cryptanalysts that take them from complete novices to experts, usually in about three years.

Given the three-year time frame for comprehensive training, it's clear that cryptanalysis is a highly-involved, demanding, and technical skill.

Fortunately for cryptanalysts, there are several trade associations available.

- International Association of Cryptologic Research (IACR)
- International Financial Cryptography Association (IFCA)
- American Crypto Association-ACA

Appendix A: DoD Approved Certifications

Information Assurance Technician (IAT) Level I	Information Assurance Technician (IAT) Level II	Information Assurance Technician (IAT) Level III
A+ CE CCNA-Security CND Network+ CE SSCP	CCNA Security CySA+ GICSP GSEC Security+ CE CND SSCP	CASP+ CE CCNP Security CISA CISSP (or Associate) GCED GCIH CCSP
Information Assurance Manager (IAM) Level I	**Information Assurance Manager (IAM) Level II**	**Information Assurance Manager (IAM) Level III**
CAP CND Cloud+ GSLC Security+ CE HCISPP	CAP CASP+ CE CISM CISSP (or Associate) GSLC CCISO HCISPP	CISM CISSP (or Associate) GSLC CCISO
Information Assurance Architect and Engineer (IASAE) I	**Information Assurance Architect and Engineer (IASAE) II**	**Information Assurance Architect and Engineer (IASAE) III**
CASP+ CE CISSP (or Associate) CSSLP	CASP+ CE CISSP (or Associate) CSSLP	CISSP-ISSAP CISSP-ISSEP CCSP
Cybersecurity Service Provider (CSSP) Analyst	**Cybersecurity Service Provider (CSSP) Infrastructure Support**	**Cybersecurity Service Provider (CSSP) Incident Responder**
CEH CFR CCNA Cyber Ops CCNA-Security CySA+ GCIA GCIH GICSP Cloud+ SCYBER PenTest+	CEH CySA+ GICSP SSCP CHFI CFR Cloud+ CND	CEH CFR CCNA Cyber Ops CCNA-Security CHFI CySA+ GCFA GCIH SCYBER PenTest+
Cybersecurity Service Provider (CSSP) Auditor	**Cybersecurity Service Provider (CSSP) Manager**	
CEH CySA+ CISA GSNA CFR PenTest	CISM CISSP-ISSMP CCISO	

Certification Provider	Certification Name
CertNexus	CyberSec First Responder (CFR)
Cisco	Cisco Certified Network Associate-Security (CCNA-Security)
	Cisco Certified Network Professional Security (CCNP Security)
	Cybersecurity Specialist Certification (SCYBER)
Computing Technology Industry Association (CompTIA)	A+ Continuing Education (CE); Cloud Plus (Cloud+)
	Security+ Continuing Education (CE)
	CompTIA Advanced Security Practitioner (CASP) Continuing Education (CE)
	Network+ Continuing Education (CE); Cybersecurity Analyst+ (CySA+)
	PenTest+
EC-Council	Certified Ethical Hacker (CEH), Certified Chief Information Security Officer (CCISO)
	Computer Hacking Forensic Investigator (CHFI), Certified Network Defender (CND)
International Information Systems Security Certifications Consortium (ISC)2	Certified Information Systems Security Professional (CISSP) (or Associate - this means the individual has qualified for the certification except for the number of years experience)
	Certified Secure Software Lifecycle Professional (CSSLP)
	Certification Authorization Professional (CAP)
	Information Systems Security Architecture Professional (ISSAP)
	Information Systems Security Engineering Professional (ISSEP)
	Information Systems Security Management Professional (ISSMP)
	Systems Security Certified Practitioner (SSCP), Certified Cloud Security Professional (CCSP)
	Health Care Information Security and Privacy Practitioner (HCISPP)
Information Systems Audit and Control Association (ISACA)	Certified Information Systems Auditor (CISA), Certified Information Security Manager (CISM)
Global Information Assurance Certification (GIAC)	GIAC Certified Enterprise Defender (GCED), GIAC Certified Forensic Analyst (GCFA)
	GIAC Certified Incident Handler (GCIH), GIAC Certified Intrusion Analyst (GCIA)
	GIAC Global Industrial Cyber Security Professional (GICSP)
	GIAC Security Essentials Certification (GSEC); GIAC Security Leadership Certificate (GSLC)
	GIAC Systems and Network Auditor (GSNA)
Logical Operations, Inc.	CyberSec First Responder (CFR)